SEEDS OF CHAOS

ROBERT M. DRAKE

OTHER BOOKS BY ROBERT M. DRAKE

Spaceship (2012)

Science (2013)

Beautiful Chaos (2014)

Black Butterfly (2015)

A Brilliant Madness (2015)

Beautiful and Damned (2016)

Broken Flowers (2016)

Gravity: A Novel (2017)

Moon Theory (2017)

For Excerpts and Updates please follow:

Instagram.com/rmdrk
Facebook.com/rmdrk
Twitter.com/rmdrk

ISBN: 978-09986293-15

Book Cover: Robert M. Drake

Cover Image licensed by Shutter Stock Inc.

For Sevyn.

All my words are yours.

CONTENTS

SEEDS OF CHAOS

ROBERT M. DRAKE

IMAGINE

She was moved by everything,

and she was beautiful.

No words could ever define
the type of love
she imagined for
herself.

SOCIETY

Society taught us how to hate.

Hate taught us violence.

Violence taught us regret.

Regret taught us pain.

Pain taught us love.

Love taught us how to laugh.

And laughter makes every moment
far more special
than we could ever imagine

for ourselves.

MAGIC

Magic is when you
live your life the way
you did not picture it
and leave nothing behind.

NO FEAR

She fell in love
like a shooting flame,
and she dreamed
between reality
and the stars
without fear.

SHE WAS

The world hated her
because they
could not
understand the science
that made her
all that
she was.

DO NOT SPEAK

The things we do not
talk about
are usually
disguised passions
for which we are not suited.

MADNESS

Madness
and chaos
are self-destructing,
but
overthinking
will always be
the suicide.

NO INTERRUPTION

You and me,
the wild air,
the naked trees,

the moon,
and not a soul
to interrupt.

EXHAUST YOURSELF

Exhaust yourself
and drift into the deepest
dream.

Escape the horrors
of reality.

Dive into the shadowy
wilderness.

Live there.
Love there.

Where all dreams are born.

BROKEN BIRTH

She was broken from
moment to moment.

Watching her world collide,
she felt lost inside herself.

She fell apart for a passion
that flamed beneath her.

She waited and died a hundred times
as the pain dripped from her pores.

And the moment she let go,
she soared over the stillness
like the star
she was born

to be.

WHAT HURTS

The truth is,
I did not need
the therapy.

I just needed to feel loved
and to know
that someone out there
craved my
attention.

That is all.

THAT NIGHT

That night,
I did not say a word.

I just watched you leave,
and in the end,
I stayed sleeping awake.

I stayed stuck,
somewhere between
a sweet dream
and a beautiful nightmare.

Hoping one day,
you would return
to rid me of all the
demons
you left behind.

DO IT

A tamed woman
will *never*
leave her mark
on the world.

And neither will
a tamed man.

Break yourself beautiful.

It is the only way to
find your perfect freedom.

LIFE IS

Life is enough to seek
the beauty in things.
But how romantic it is,
knowing that one day
we will perish
and leave nothing behind

but

our memories,
to linger
in the hearts
of those we had
the blessing to touch.

PASS THAT

The greatest
adventure is

to have no fear
to have no regret
to have no lust

for the blaze
that lies ahead.

NO HATE HERE

Hate me.
Hate me all you want,

for hate
is all that you desire.

Hate is all that you wish for,

all you want to grasp,

but you
have not.

THE CHAOS

She needed the chaos
within her,
in order to
discover the extraordinary
that no man
could ever reach.

Stay classy.

LIFE FOREVER

It was a dying art,
the way he stayed awake,
watching her dream
beneath the blinking
stars.

THE INFINITE LOOP

Art breeds love,
and still, art is birthed
by pain.

Feel this pain,
these words that do not
please the whole.

I find serenity in brokenness.
I find genius.
I find heart.
I find tears
and blood.

This is my art and
the best way I know
to cure my pain.

BROKEN BEING

She was not broken.

She was bent,
and it was over the chance
of being ignored
by the one
she truly loved.

ONE NIGHT

She got inside me
with her story.

I could feel her flowing
in me, and from afar,
we related in parallel.

Her pain was my pain.
Her tears were my tears,

and together we rode the night
into divine darkness.

Her smile was a reflection
of my brokenness.

It defined buried
feelings
I could never ignore.

ALONE

Maybe one day,

we will find that place
where you and I
can be together,

and we will catch our
dreams within the
waves of change.

So hear me—

you are not alone.

LIE BY ME

Lie by my side in silence.
Words need not be mentioned.

I, too, yearn for your company
and no wander in this place
could forbid us what this is,
what we have.

I am yours and you are mine.

So let the force of us
thunder these walls

and let us create
something the world
has never witnessed.

Two moons colliding.
Two wishes
becoming true.

WHAT I NEED

I need you
because I know
I deserve you,
but let me fall in love
with you
one last time
before I go.

I need to remember
the imperfection
that rattled
my bones.

WHAT WE DO NOT KNOW

We are the society
we so desperately blame
for all
our faults
buried beneath our
scars.

A WEAPON

Use love
as the only
instrument
to question
the world
around you.

So find it,
because God hides it
in the most unusual of places.

Let it wave through
the breath of new
beginnings.

DREAMER

She was a beautiful dreamer.

She was the kind of girl
who kept her head
in the clouds,
loved above the stars,
and left regret
beneath the earth
she walked on.

I LOVED HER

She had more of me
than I had of myself,
and it was as if
we were two wild birds
chasing the moon.

We would always lose our way
to find new places.

We would close our eyes
and fall backward toward
a constellation of dreams.

We wrapped ourselves
in a blanket of passion,
and each night we fell
deeper and deeper
without control.

She had me,
and together
we found ourselves in this
strange world
called love.

THE TRUTH

With all honesty,
somewhere between
the hello
and the dreams, I saw you and
I fell in love.

What a beautiful life
in which to wake up.

Thank you
for the inspiration,
the love,
and the fire to keep going.

EVERY HOUR

I kept loving
and loving
and loving.

Every waking hour,
I marveled at the hours,
the moments,
that made me feel.

I want to love the world
and be the change
it needs.

TIGHT PLACES

It was never about
the world being too big.

It was more like
she was too much
for the world to handle.

WE ARE

We are only
instruments of love

flowing through heaps
of pain

in hopes that maybe,
one day,

someone will grab us
by the hand

and tell us that our faults
still make us beautiful.

I DID NOT KNOW

Appreciate the moment
of a first kiss.
It may be the last time
you own your heart.

SAVE

Maybe
love is meant
to save us
from ourselves.

SHE HAD

She had the power
to change the world,

but she could not
save the one she loved.

Sometimes the most
beautiful people
are beautifully broken

THE LAST HOUR

At the end of the day,
I went to this place
where memories of you
left footprints on my skin
and the breath of your
touch stained my desire.

Yes, it was one of those
nights when I needed
you the most.

THE CHILDREN

We swallowed the chaos
because we knew
we did not
want to be ordinary.

EYES LOCKED

I think
that when I met you,
I became myself again
and we stumbled
toward this world
and made sense of it

together.

IN THE MORNING

Suddenly
I remembered that laugh,
and it told a different story,

our story.

BROKEN BROKEN

I wrote her story because
she wanted to live forever,
and I loved her
far more with every word.

She was the book that
I was too afraid to write.

HOPE

Maybe I hope too much.

Maybe I dream too much.

Or maybe

I love too much
to just give up on you.

MAYBE

Maybe all that we are
is what people expect us
to be,

or

maybe we are more,
but we expect
much less
than we think
we deserve.

DRUG

Excuse me.
I feel interrupted,
and I think
I have overdosed
on the idea
of loving you.

IT COULD BE

Maybe what this is,

what we have,

is

something that
will save us
from ourselves.

TREES BURN

She wildly burned
for the one
she loved,

and he stood there
watching her,

hoping that maybe
one day
he would be able to catch
a blaze
from the violence
stirring
within her
heart.

FRAGILE WORLD

Society
will always be
too fragile
to accept us
for all
that makes us
beautiful.

CLOUDS

I know how you feel
because I have been there.

I have hated, and I have loved.

I have seen my demons root
and crawl
and my angels branch
and soar.

I have died within myself,
and I have lived a thousand
different lives.

I, too, fight the war,
and I, too, am drowning
in the puddles
of self-consciousness
this world has created.

ROCKET SHIPS

The more I learned,
the less I felt.

I got lost counting stars.
I fell dreaming.

And sometimes, I would wander away.

Maybe I was not ready,
or maybe it was just a hard time
to love.

But you always reminded me of home,
and I could never fathom
the reasoning behind
your smile.

Perhaps, one day,
if we believe enough,

we will find our way

back to where we belong.

THE LANDING

I arrived.
I saw the humans,
and I saw through
their faces.

Nothing ever seems to change
but the light in their eyes.

For I, too, have buried
demons today,
without knowing
what might remain
beneath the face of tomorrow.

The pain is buried,
but it is never meant
to go away.

DARKNESS

It is dark,
and I am reading my scars
because our moments
remind me
of where I should be.

Sometimes the past
reveals the future,
and sometimes the future
means nothing at all.

SIMPLE

Death is the easy part.
The hard part is living
and knowing that
you could be so much
more than you are
willing to be.

The mirror never lies,
and you should look at
yourself more often.

Your eyes,
your smile,
your happiness

will always lead
the way.

STEW BOY

The fear of loving a dog is
knowing that one day,
it will be gone
and you will never again
find eyes
that express
all that you feel.

SUNSHINE

You are not a bad person.
You are just a little
bit different,
and I have always been
a sucker for that.

SLUMBER

Your greatest dreams
will always slumber
within
the vicious depths
of fear.

Wake up.
Today everything
could be yours.

BELIEVE

She dreamed in color
and designed a world
for herself
where love was
inevitable.

LOVE YOU DEEPLY

I will love you
with every bit of everything
that has ever consumed me.

And I will, forever,
love you in every life
and so forth.

I will love you
until the stars die above
the horizon
and the universe leaps
into the nothingness.

I will love you,
and deeply I will
until nothing remains.

NO PLACE

She was broken,
and it wasn't because the
world hated her
or because sometimes she
felt out of place.

It was because she loved too much,
and she was always
blind to the fact

that love,
too,
is

sometimes broken.

SHORES

Bring me back.
Save me from all that
I have become.

All this pain,
this suffering.

Save me.

Let me become the things
you love.

Let me find my way,
but only if it is with you.

Save me with your kiss,
your touch.

Save me, soft in the warmth of your arms.

Let your dreams drift toward my shore
and let them rest upon
the sand

forever.

I KNOW I KNOW

The best kind
of humans
are the ones
who stay.

A PLACE FOUND

The chaos in me
is the chaos in you,
like the love in me
is the love in you.

So maybe we are both
a little crazy,

crazy enough to believe
we have found
where dreams are born.

And somewhere, beneath
our errors and our faults
and what hurts,

this place
is the only place
to which you and I
will run away.
And when we do,
we will leave nothing
behind.

ILLUSIONS

But dear,
do not be afraid
of love.
It is,
after all,
only magic.

BRIGHT

Suddenly
everything was bright.

Everything was soft
and beautiful,
for the way she began
to view the world
was nothing more
than a reflection
of herself.

And it was funny,
for all it took was
a broken heart.
That alone was enough
for her to do everything
she had ever dreamed
of.

MILLION LIVES

If I had lived
a million lives,

I would have felt
a million
feelings,
and I still
would have fallen
a million times
for you.

EVERY DAY

This life,
all that we are,
every day,
we are closer to
our doom.

And somewhere
between life
and death,

we must find
the space
for all
that makes us
special.

ONE SECOND LATER

Sometimes
to self-discover
you must
self-destruct.

DISSOLVE

I had to learn
to live without you,

and I could never
make sense of it

because I had left
so much of me
inside of you.

The world moves
backward
and the hours
dissolve
without you.

WHERE IT BEGINS

How could I live above the water
or breathe beneath it?

How could I swim in total darkness
or be consumed in an ocean of you?

Falling or flying toward you,
losing or finding myself in you?

Beauty was never the word
to catch all that you are,
what we are,

for now I know the means
of the infinite.

It all starts and ends
with you.

THE SHATTERING

To be human
is to be broken,
and broken
is its own kind of
beautiful.

ALONG THE PATH

Somewhere
along the way,
we all go a bit mad.

So burn,
let go and dive into the horror,

because maybe it is
the chaos
that helps us find

where we belong.

FOREVER

Forever does not seem
too far away.

Sometimes it is after
we have lost someone that
we learn how to love.

Where hope
and dreams greet each other
and everything is beautifully
perfect,
the way it was meant to be.

So hear me.
Soon enough
we will meet again,

old friend.

DIFFERENCES

Do not worry,
little heart.

They are only feelings.

So care a little
less,

and the ride will be
much more
than what it seems.

TELESCOPES

Look deeper
through the telescope

and

do not be afraid
when the stars collide
toward the darkness,

because sometimes

the most marvelous
things

begin

in chaos.

MAPS UNKNOWN

Sweet child,

but we are all
lost here.

So close those eyes
and follow
where your heart
leads.

THE NEED

All she needed
was a little push
to feather into
the arms
of the one
she truly loved.

I WANT US

I want us
to fall in love
like drops of rain.

Grow in it like
we grow through life.

I want us to never
look back,
like we left nothing behind.

I want us
together
forever,
floating intertwined
through the black clouds
and the bright skies.

I want us.
You and me,
till the end of time.

GRAB THE SKY

Your sky
is full of stars
and my arms
are too short
to reach a piece
of you
to claim
as my very own.

RETURN TO BLACK

Things were falling apart.
We just could not slow down.
We were evolving into
something greater,
perhaps even
too good for our own good.

But as we left each other behind,
one thing always remained
as I moved on.

I saved a little bit of love
just in case
you ever
decided to return
home.

BEAUTIFUL CHAOS

Come away with me.
Let us go somewhere,
you and me,
just the two of us.

Let us wander away
like paper bags
through the darkness.

Let us forget our worries
and do all things today

that

will help build a better
tomorrow.

WHAT CAN HAPPEN

Always explore the world
with new eyes,

dream of places you have
never imagined,

and discover a love
so perfect,
it was almost not meant
to be.

STRANDS OF HAIR

Every night
I was going back
to the strands of our
memories,

and some nights
I would surrender
to the fabric of you.

One night is never enough.

I will always want
you a little more.

LIONS AND WOLVES

She slept with the
wolves
without fear,
for the wolves
knew a lioness
was among them.

DRIFT DRIFT

Drift,
drift away
and never return
to the norm.

And when you do
come back,
never,
never drift toward
the shores
of the
ordinary.

BETWEEN THE SPACE

Look between the spaces.
Come lie next to me.

Now listen closely.

I need you to touch me
like you own me.

Dive into my skin
and force me to surrender.

Make me forget my name
and make me remember only
yours.

Lift me in the air, so I can
crash toward the clouds,
to land in your arms.

Now look into the space inside
my eyes
and find the heat that scorched
this interest
so passionately toward you.

I love you.

EMPTY BED

Sometimes
your side of the bed
tells a certain kind of story,

where your body would slumber
and leave trenches
within the bedsheets.

Well, sometimes
I memorize each crevice.

And sometimes
I even close my eyes
and run my fingers through
them.

It is memories of you
that come and
lie with me
during the times when
I am filled with too many
of these empty
spaces.

BUTTERFLY

You float
through my world
leaving trails
of color
through my skies.

WEEP WEEP

What if a shy hello
would spark a blaze?

I stand firm, being still.

All while I wait
for a glance of attention,
of notice.

Her voice
like keys, and my lust
like the moon,
rising over the scape
where the lost ones go,
the mad ones.

I thirst for her touch, her feeling
before my tired eyes
and stand alone.

You pass, and I,
like the classic fool,
believe in dreams.

I weep for a lost
love so deep
that has yet to happen.

MOMENTS IN TIME

I loved
the way she
spoke
while she
stared
at the stars.

STOLEN HEART

She stole my breath
when I was willing to surrender it.
She had it all.
Everything the universe created
revolved around her.

She had too much force, gravity,
and every day she drew me in
closer and closer.

Until forever fades away and there
is nothing left
but the black of dead space.

She stood before me
with her heart so open,
flowers would fall out
as it pumped.

I love her in all her glory,
but she left just as fast as she arrived.

A star that's shooting,
roaring through the sky,

and I,
here alone, typing these words
I've known I have not
the heart to say.

SHE PART ONE

She was fierce.
She was strong.
She was not simple.
She was crazy,
and sometimes she barely slept.

She always had something to say,
and she had flaws,
but that too was okay.

When she was down,
she got right back up.

She was a beast
in her own way,
but one idea described her best:

She was unstoppable
and she took anything
she wanted,
with a smile.

WHEN DEATH COMES

We were doomed
from the very start.
And what a tragic
foreshadowing it is,

for we have all
fallen in love with life,
one way or another.

Time passes, and clocks
eat themselves,

and soon afterward,
death comes into the room,
grinning, lurking,
knowing that one day

it will divorce you from me
and keep life
and us
separated forever.

KISS ME

Kiss
like it is lost
forever,
and
love
like the first time

you looked
into my eyes.

WHY

There she was,
staring at the
television static
with a blank face.

Her bruised lips
stained a barely lit cigarette.

Slightly tilted,
she felt a push
coming from the waves,
the voices
telling her she was not
beautiful.

And she knew she was
not perfect,
but she also knew she was different
inside.

She had wounds deep enough
to swallow the city.

Do not rape me again,

she thought as the blood of rage
covered her flesh
and the light in
her eyes suddenly became
black.

WHY WHAT?

In the stillness
of the night,
she stood in darkness
and colored
the street
with nothing more
than a smile.

LETTERS

I wrote her letters
using my typewriter,
and she wrote me letters
using her heart.

DEFEAT AND THINGS

She defeated
the demons
beneath her skin,
but she
could never rid herself of
the demons
buried within her
bones.

DREAM COLOR

We are together
day by day, people
leaving their bones
in the care of other people.

We are separated
night by night,
gathering all that
we can from those
who keep passing
by.

Our beauty
inspires God
to keep dreaming
in color.

SHE LEFT

She left.
She found a way out.
She never returned
to those who had destroyed
her.

Believe that the sky
speaks to people,

because

change was among
the stars
the moment she began
to love
herself
for who she was.

NO WORDS GIVEN

Somewhere
along the way,
I drifted into something
I could never put
into words.

FLOWERS

Roots grow
from the bottom
and leaves bloom
from the top.

I see. I see. I see.

We are all
flowers,
waving underneath
the starry stars.

MY DEAR

My dear,
every unread letter
I wrote to you
had a piece of my soul.

A memory
that reminded me

of how special
we could have been.

RUBBLE

In the chaotic rubble,
she remembered
who she was.

And he remembered
everything he wanted.

And together they lived their lives
without meeting each other.

What a terrible way
to breathe.

IN WONDERLAND

She slugged her heart
toward these cracked
walls,
and in an instant
it shattered.

That was the beginning
of her adventure.

Her heart ran off,
and she had no choice
but to chase it.

DREAM AWAKE

Dream with the dreamers
and invent things you never
knew you had in you.
Think with the thinkers
and discover ideas that
mold who you are.
Smile at strangers
and make friends who
will last a lifetime.
Laugh often and let
those memories burn
through your heart.
Travel with travelers
and explore a life beyond
your imagination.
Love only one
and grow old with your best
friend.

Let these things bring fire
to your soul, so that when you look
back at your life, you will
have no regrets.

And you could leave this
place better
than how you found it.

Amen.

AFRAID TO SWIM

To grasp
the depth of love,

we must
always
risk the monstrous
grin
of hatred.

HORRORS RISING

Her horrors
were the remains
of a pain
that shook her life.

She dragged
herself out of the water,

interrupted by
everything that moved her.

She rises,
and when she does,
the world rises as well.

She is all sun
and all moon,
and when she walks,

she lights all that can be
seen.

IGNORED

The most
precious moments
in life
are usually
ignored,

and the most
ignored moments
in life
are often lost
in a blink
of an eye.

WIND LIES

The wind whispered
a destructive history that
I wanted to forget.

But every time
your name would float
above my ears,

my heart's waves
would clash.

If I say
I do not miss you,
then
I am a liar.

And liars die every night
and rise every morning
to face
what isn't truly there.

COLD MONSTER

She did not move.

Inside she burned alive.

Slowly opened her mouth
and from the pits,
she revealed her soul.

Eyes black.
Lungs black.
Blood black.

With a cold stare,
she spoke:

"I am all things
that light cannot touch.
I am all things that
devour the world."

The light dims,
and the sound slowly
fades into

oblivion.

THE BRAKES

The moon within
your eyes has
swallowed the sky.

And the fabric
of your soul
has gently
covered the light.

I am blind.
I am in love.

If I cannot see,
then I will crash.

And I see you
before me,
and I have no
idea

how the brakes
work.

GOD KNOWS

And then
God slightly smiled.

And he did so
because he knew

that we had no
clue
how closely
we were drawn
to each other.

BONES AND SOULS

From this pain,
we grow scars
to hide what is
beneath our souls

and stay interrupted
from a reality
that lies within
our empty bones.

SHE LET HERSELF

She did not care
about the broken heart.
She cared about the way
she surrendered herself.

She never imagined
this love would destroy her.

She fell over her past
and thought, *How could
this have happened?*

Things happen.
Love happens.

And in the end,
she had the courage
to look far away
and let herself burn
for the one
she loved.

IMAGINE IF I

Imagine
if I fell apart.

If I melted
all over you.

Over your body,
your heart.

Imagine this.
Imagine our bodies
becoming one,
becoming something
we cannot understand.

Imagine your soul
combined with mine.

Together we are
sun and earth,
and we need each other
to go on.

MY SCARS

My scars remind me
of where I have been.

And your scars remind
me of how perfect
you really are.

ACHING TO BE

I hugged you until
you melted right through
my arms.

I watched you drip
away onto the pavement
of nothingness,

where dreams
go to die.

And the ghost of your future
passed right by me
with a darkness so bright
that it dissolved into my heart.

I cannot sleep.
You are in my very soul,

aching to come out.
Aching to tell me
what we should have become.

TOO BEAUTIFUL

She wrapped herself
in attention, and she
soaked herself with a
suspicious beauty
too precious to ignore.

She is glorious,
like ten thousand suns
above the sky.

She is all we wish to see.

All things too beautiful,
and all things the average
person ignores.

RAIN FALLS

We swept
across dreams
like the rain.

We drowned
both of our demons.

We rested our heavy
hearts in the puddles
we created.

If I am the rain,
then you are the rain.

Together we will drown
the world.

We are the storms that
we have tried to convince
our hearts
aren't really
there.

EMPTY ROOMS

An empty room
would still be a beautiful
place,
if only the
memory of you
crowded my heart.

YOUR EYES

Your eyes
always carried
a certain kind
of story,
a mayhem of words.

Misunderstood.

And I
was married to
every sentence,
because, as always,

you devoured me
from the start.

Time keeps going,
but the world will
one day end.

YOUR EYES BLOOM

Your eyes bloom.
They are a window
into your soul.

And I can see
the pain,
the hurting.

Loving you
is not easy,

but every time
you look me in the
eyes,

you grow more beautiful.

Pain makes you stronger,
and the stronger you are,

the more precious
you become.

FOUND ME

I have been searching for
my entire life,

through every crack,
under every rock.

I flipped the entire
globe upside down
searching for
something,
something I have
never seen.

And in the darkest hour,
I surrendered.
I gave up.

And that was when

YOU

found me.

BEATING

And the sky
smiled right
back at you,

like it knew
a little more
about you

each night.

CHAOS CHAOS

Your gorgeous chaos
was a danger
to my ordinary life.

I knew this,
and knew this,

and still,
as the wind
flowed and pushed
the sky,

we became
extraordinary.

Together
we became more.

Sometimes
we don't become
special
until we feel
the burn of love.

LOVING YOU

If loving you
kills me tonight,

then

I was ready for death
the moment
you said
hello.

GONE MAD

The people want more
but do not know what
to do with more.

The people want love
but do not know
what to do with love.

The people want peace
but still crave war.

We have all gone
beautifully mad
in a beautifully mad
world.

REMEMBER

Remember the night when

you dissolved into
the air
and told me
to take a deep
breath and inhale
you?

I've been holding
my breath ever since.

BATTERED

Her eyes are
like a battered
black sun.

She remembers
the suffering
the world caused.

In her soul
slumbers
a killer's instinct.

She keeps going.
She does not end.

She's a wolf
and she will not
stop
until life is
at the mercy
at her fangs.

LAYERS OF PAIN

She painted
beneath the break
of tears
and underneath
the layers of
pain,

the sound of her
rain
carrying a sweet
tune
worth loving.

It was her faults
that made her
interesting
and who she was.

WAVES AND WORDS

She smiled
at the ocean
because the
waves
told her
story.

STUMBLING

We are all
stumbling in the
dark,
but
we are far too
close to
the light
to remain still.

BEAUTIFUL WOMAN

And the stitches
across her chest
defined her
past.

So she presented
her heart,
like some beautiful
woman
no man could
ever resist.

MADNESS IS

Madness
is somewhere
between
chaos and
having a
dream.

LOVE IS

Love is
a touch of
friendship
and a
handful
of dreams.

SADNESS AGAIN

You
can never
recognize
happiness,
if you have
ever danced
the night away
with sorrow.

TO LET

To let
yourself
go
is to
burn
with desire
and never
look back.

UNTAMABLE LOVE

I want to lie beneath
whatever comes after.
I want to feather within
your heart and howl
deep enough
to awaken all that you are.
I want to pour out
the moons and the skies
to create worlds
forgotten by the stars.
I want to land softly
in your arms, land softly
in your thoughts.
I want you and I
to hunt this untamable
animal called love.
I want to conquer it
until there is nothing
left except the puddle
of dreams we created.

This love
is nothing more
than a game.

One
that is never
in our favor.

SLUMBER, PLEASE

Sometimes
your greatest
dreams
are the ones
your heart
slumbers.

TODAY'S DAY

Society pushes us
to pour out
our beauty
and uniqueness

so it can
bury us alive
for being too
different.

DEMONS AND SADNESS

Sad girl,
it is okay to cry.

For I, too,
know what it is
like
to bury demons
alive,

knowing that one day soon,
they will
crawl back out.

BORN WITH BULLETS

Trust is the
only weapon
in the chaos
of love.

VIOLENT SEA

What is beneath
defines us,
and maybe I have
seen too much
darkness to ignore
the dimmest shine

buried underneath
those lonely eyes.

I feel you.

Sadness is an ocean,
and sometimes
we drown,
while at other times
we are forced
to swim.

DEAR GOD

Dear God,
I am not like you.
I am weak, my bones
are brittle, and my heart
is filled with darkness.

At times, my demons
crawl out from behind the walls
you helped me build.

I am an extension of you,
but what would it be like to be
away in the ocean of you?

To be lost in your shine
and drown in your brilliance?

So maybe I have ignored you
for the past few years, and like you,
I, too, seek the beauty
in humanity.

So hear me:
you are not alone.

RID ME

Rid me of all that has ruined me.

Rid me of this darkness that clings to my heart.

Rid me of this brokenness, this
wholeness. Rid me of all the things
that fill me empty.

Rid me in pieces. Rid me to nothing,
but leave a bit of me to grow.

Rid me to rid me in you,
and not a second less,

to fill me with all that makes you
expand in such a small space.

So that the best of me spills
over you
and leaves not a trace to spoil.

FOREVER CYCLE

I will be your spring
if you will be my summer.

I will be your fall
if you will be my winter.

And we will cycle
and cycle
and cycle,
until forever breaks
the seconds
and the seconds
define us

for every moment
we spend.

LEAVE BEHIND

Maybe
we are too human,
and disaster
trails behind us.

And I never,
for the life of me,
understood us.

For how could something
so beautiful cause
us so much pain?

The more we give,
the more we take,
and none of us
take a minute to think

of how empty
we feel
as we give each other
all we've ever had.

Love leaves you broken,
and sometimes there are
no pieces left behind.

FIRE IN THE MIND

She said
I had a way with
words,
and I said
she had a way
with laughter.

It spoke to me
the way imagination
speaks to a child.

Inspiring.

MIRRORS

Sometimes
you have to shatter
the mirror in you

to see all the pieces
that make you
beautiful.

BROKE BEAUTIFUL

I broke myself
beautiful when I left
you.

It was me
saving me
from myself.

FROM THE START

You said your heart
had been broken,
and I believed enough that
we would be forever.

Well, I guess history
has a funny way
of repeating itself.

And it is a shame
how everything meaningful
must end,

how everything happens
for a reason,

and how two people
who once shared a bed

are now oceans from each other,
wondering

how their lives got to this point
from the start.

CONQUER

Conquer the demons
in yourself
before letting
the demons in others
conquer you.

CREATED LIES

Be authentic
to yourself.
But if you must
cheat,
then cheat yourself
out of the lies
the world created.

STILL FLAMES

I am slowly falling
apart, scorching away,

and my ashes drizzle,
and I have destroyed
myself once again

to wind over your shores.

To remind you
that there is
someone out there
who still
burns for you.

AND LOVING YOU

And loving you
was a pattern of
self-discovery,
because some way,

somehow,

I always ended up
learning something
new about myself.

MILLION PIECES

I would break into
a million pieces,

if only it meant
a million pieces
of me

to call your own.

WITHOUT WAKE

I was married to the idea
of loving her.

She sold it well, and the
words "I love you"
felt like being burned
alive, and it hurt,

but I swallowed the pain
over and over
to slumber in the field
of her.

Without waking,

I found myself dreaming.

Dreaming of how
my world without her
would be too incomplete

as I kept throwing
my heart toward a sun
I knew
I couldn't reach.

BURNS AND LIFE

There is a charge in me
that burns for you.

I crave to recover all of you,
all the pieces, and peel away
all that sours you.

So do not be afraid
when I give you all of my years,
my hours,
and my seconds,

because

every moment spent finding you
will be every moment
spent finding myself.

The more I breathe you in,
the more my lungs
fill my body
with all the things
I need to go on.

SHE WENT ON

She went on
and became too
human.

She alone
accepted all of her
faults,

and in the end,
she was good.

Everything that
happened was enough
to keep her smiling
permanently.

SUNSETS FALL

It kills me
that you linger so close,

and because of it,

I will never be at ease
while watching the sunset,

knowing

that our stories will never end
with the same words.

Every sunset has its
own story.

It is just

that our sun will always
set incompletely.

TALK DIRTY

A touch of madness
will always be
stored in the crater
of love.

MAGIC MOMENT

And every
magic moment
brought her
closer
to her dreams.

Because all she needed
was a minute
to fall in love with
the stars,

and after that night,
everything changed.

She believed in herself.

She believed in love,
and she chose
to find it,
no matter what
the world said.

MYSELF SOMETIMES

Sometimes,

I feel like I do not know myself,

like I am lost inside myself.

And I cannot live within myself,
and I cannot trust myself
when I am by myself.

Too many broken pieces of myself,

too empty, and maybe I am not myself.

I think I need you to save me
from myself,
because without you,
I am just not myself.

DANGER

Danger will always
chase her,
and she will always
greet it
with a smile.

PLEASE UNDERSTAND

Please understand,
that without you, I
cannot finish the day.

I cannot rest buried only
in the light, for I, too,
need darkness in order to close
my eyes and dream.

I, too, need the stars
to lamp over my tired eyes.

I cannot find the words
to describe why I need you.

I need you like a poor man
needs a dream.

That alone is enough
to define everything of everything

of all the things
I have kept buried for so long.

The moon needs to come out,
and it needs to shed comfort
on those who sing the same song.

LOVE YOU TODAY

You will always be
beautiful,
before and after today,

and when our days
have seen age,

all that once was
will always remain.

Sometimes love is
a silly little thing.
It comes and goes,

but the memories
stay.

IMAGINE ALL

Imagine
what we would
accomplish,
together,
if we left our egos
at the door.

What a different
world it would be.

What a beautiful
place to call home.

SHE SAID, HE SAID

She said
she loved the ocean,
and I said
I loved the stars,

and for the first time,
we agreed on something.

We both saw ourselves
loving the things
about which we dreamed
and ignoring
everything

that made us beautiful.

A LITTLE MORE

Laugh a little more,
care a little more,
and love a little more.

For all we will ever be
is all that we become.

And in the end,

we become all the things
we leave behind.

We become memories
and ghosts,
and none of them
were meant to be held.

Both dissolve into the air,
as we see them vanish
from our hands.

LET US

Let us go to a place
where no one knows us
and find our smiles.

Let us go to a place
where we can wander
and find our laugher.

Let us go to a place
where we can find ourselves
and find innocence.

Let us go to a place
where we can fall
and find a love to catch us

and take us to a place
where only fools
rush in.

MAYBE THE WORLD

Maybe all the
broken dreams
and empty promises
the world offers
are just reflections
of what is within us.

Maybe one day

we will learn to accept
ourselves for all the
faults sleeping beneath
the footsteps
we leave behind.

I DON'T WANT TO

I know it is late,
but come away with me.

Let us run away
in the dark,
and I promise you

I will never see
myself without you

again

and again

and again.

I don't want to see
the world without you.

KNOWING IT

We all could be great
and leave our dreams
on the shore.

Drift away and still
believe the best is yet to come.

And even after everything,
even after the tide brings
us back to where we end,

I would still feel empty,
knowing

we drifted apart
and you were only
an ocean away
from being where you
belonged.

MADE SENSE

She always felt lost,
and it was rather beautiful
not knowing how she
would find herself.

For everything she knew
was a speck of something
great,

and

it was just a matter of time
until all of her
made sense.

THE WORK IN

He returned to her,
and his lips awakened
every atom in her body.

His love exhausted
her stars.

She could not help
the change.

She stumbled,

lost her balance,

wrapped herself
in his moonlight,

and

forever seasoned
his love.

HER STORY

Maybe her story
does not have an ending.

Maybe God will
remember her
and wheel her through
the air,

so that we can all breathe
her in
and exhale her brilliance
into the wind.

WE ARE

We are beautiful
things,
wild things,

searching for the
brilliance within us.

MISSING YOU

'Cause missing you
feels like the sunset,
and not a night
goes by
when I don't walk toward
the shore,

wishing that one day,

you will shipwreck
and finally
stay home.

WILLING TO LET

There was too much inside us.

Maybe it was love,
or maybe it was something else.

We had a light, a connection
that we tried so hard to ignore.

And all our mistakes
had little significance
for the story
of which we were not willing
to let go.

DEAR GOD II

Dear God,

Every gust of wind
carries your voice.
Every sunrise radiates
the warmth derailing
from your smile.
Every ocean reflects
the shades, seasoning
from your eyes
and during the night
I can see everything
you have ever wanted to see
in me.
Every mountain
and meadow reminds me
of your scripting skin.
And I know that you, too, feel
broken at times.

I know because we all have
a piece of you inside us.

We all reflect our makers
and become like those
who made us
who we are.

EXPLODE SKY

One day

someone will inspire you,
and a love will chalk
over your walls,
and the sun will love you
and follow you.

You will walk in sunshine.

And you, too,

will inspire and continue
to be inspired,
and you will never
destroy these moments
where you and the light
meet.

You will never end.

The love stored inside you
will explode
to taint the sky.

BECOME IT

The more
she went on
to forget love,

the closer
she went on
to become it.

AIR DAYS

In your voice,
I can hear a hundred
years of music,

a thousand years
of stars colliding,
and a million years
of everything beyond.

Pulsating through the
vibrations of your soul,

I have been listening
to the way you have come
together.

And now I understand
why we are vessels submerged
in pain, in love.

Because I have always drowned
in you, and forever I will run

to the only place I know
I can breathe.

You give me air
when no one else is around.

DEEP OCEANS

We all can learn
how to breathe submerged.

We just have to find
that one person
worth drowning for.

THE DAYS GO

Stop looking for something
when something has
already found you.

You have been living
with your eyes closed.

Awaken.
It is there.

Take it,

because it is yours.

WHERE WE STAND

We are
ninety-three
million miles
from the sun,
two hundred
and thirty-eight
thousand miles
from the moon.

A moment
from finding magic,
and one kiss away
from reaching
our dreams.

COLLIDE

You will be the clouds
and I will be the sky.

You will be the ocean
and I will be the shore.

You will be the trees
and I will be the wind.

You will be the stars
and I will be the moon.

You will be the sunset
and I will be the horizon.

Whatever we are,

you and I
will always collide.

KEEP IT SIMPLE

Keep your smile
youthful,
and never let go
when the wind
calls your name.

And let your love
flow where the
beautiful things are,
and something beautiful
will always come
your way.

LOVE HATE

Maybe I love
too much
and show it
too little.

ROCK IT

We are like astronauts:

dreaming on the moon,

telescoping the stars,

exploring the skies,

and searching for
the moments
that take
our breath away.

WISHING OF YOU

Somewhere,
someone is thinking
of you.

Wishing that someday,
somewhere,
.somehow,
you will meet.

TOO MANY LITTLE

She destroyed herself,
too many little thoughts.

She wrote herself,
too many little words.

She lost herself,
too many little places.

She fell in love,
too many little feelings.

She discovered herself,
too many little stars.

She believed,
too many little moments.

And in the end,

she was home,
too many little things
that reminded her
of her life.

FREEDOM

You are only
as free
as you think
you are,

and

freedom
will always be
as real
as you believe
it to be.

TRADE SPOTS

I taught her
how to dream,
and she taught
me how to love,

and

we saved
each other,
the moment
we began
to believe.

LEARN SOMETHING

Do not promise
her the stars
if you cannot
see them yourself,

and

never tell her
you love her
if love
does not mean
the world to you.

IS A SMILE

One day,
you will make
peace with your demons,

and the chaos
in your heart
will settle flat.

And maybe
for the first time
in your life,

life will smile
right back at you

and welcome
you home.

COLORS FOR BLIND

Those eyes
have seen so many
places,
and that heart
has felt so many
things,

and yet

you still smile
at the darkest
of feelings
and find expression
in all
that is colored
beautiful.

I BELONG

We cannot deny
the brilliance
rooted deeply
within us

and these moments
that break us
and introduce us
to something
beyond the ordinary.

Love hides in all places,

and sometimes

you find me
to bring me back

where I belong.

SHE WAS OR IS

She was a lot
like the ocean.

She was a lot
like the wind
and the stars.

She taught me
how to drown

and feel things
above the sky.

TODAY IT ENDS

If loving you
kills me tonight,

then I was
ready for death

the moment

you said hello.

SORRY I FEEL IT

Sometimes
I do not feel,
and sometimes,
I think
too differently.

I do not belong
because I cannot
find myself.

And I am sorry that
my heart is not
big enough for you
to call it home,

when I cannot
even say that
for myself.

WHAT TO DO?

If we move too fast,
we will break things.

If we move too slowly,
we will miss things.

And if
we do not move at all,

we will not see things
for how beautiful
they truly are.

HOLD ON TO

Maybe tomorrow
that goodbye
will lead to a new
hello,

and maybe this time
you will fuel
the fire in her
heart and make
her stay.

WE ARE MAGIC

We are magic.

We are moments.

We are dreams
and we are memories.

We are everything.

And in the depths,
we swim deeper to discover
that we are not born whole,
so we cannot be broken.

We are born in twos,
and we are searching
for the other piece,

that other person
to guide us home.

TODAY IS ALMOST GONE

But there is
so much to smile
about,

so why waste
your time
wiping away
all of those
tears?

YOU

There is too much
noise in me,
and too often
I feel interrupted.

I need order.
I need love.

I need all of you
to calm the waves.

All of you
to set me free,
and all of you

for all of me.

SAVE US

To save us
from them,

we must
separate ourselves.

And to be different,

we must question
everything
that makes us
who we are.

SHE GOES ON

There is too much fuel in her.
The world ignites her fire
and she works both ways.

When she loves,
she loves too much.
And when she hates,
she hates too much.

And in between
there is so much rage,
so much that she loses
herself in those moments.

And the closer she gets,
the further apart she is.

She cannot get it together.

Time flows,
and birds sing,

and she finds her way
as she goes on.

HATE IS HEAVY

I need you
to understand
that hate is heavy,
so put it down.

Burn it down,
all of it,
and leave regret
beneath its ashes.

So that when the fire
in your heart sparks,

everything you do
will burn bright
and hot.

The world will never
cease to ignore
the stars in you.

LEAVE YOUR HEART

She left her heart little.
She left her heart childish.

And for her,
every moment felt
like butterflies.

She did not want
to believe there was
an end to love.

So she drowned
in the seconds beneath
the moments
where magic and stillness
collide.

And every time
she looked into her
own eyes,

she was reminded
of how strong she was
from the start.

She was all ocean,
and life was the shore
too small to
catch her waves.